# KILLER (THEROPOD) DINOSAURS



DINO-SORTED!

CLASSIFY THE FEATURES OF PREHISTORIC CREATURES

IZZI HOWELL

Gareth Stevens PUBLISHING

**Please visit our website, www.garethstevens.com. For a free color catalog of all our high-quality books, call toll free 1-800-542-2595 or fax 1-877-542-2596.**

**Cataloging-in-Publication Data**
Names: Howell, Izzi.
Title: Killer dinosaurs / Izzi Howell.
Description: Buffalo, NY : Gareth Stevens Publishing, 2026. | Series: Dino-sorted! | Includes glossary and index.
Identifiers: ISBN 9781482473667 (pbk.) | ISBN 9781482473674 (library bound) | ISBN 9781482473681 (ebook)
Subjects: LCSH: Saurischia--Juvenile literature. | Saurischia--Classification--Juvenile literature.
Classification: LCC QE862.S3 N483 2026 | DDC 567.912--dc23

Published in 2026 by
**Gareth Stevens Publishing**
2544 Clinton St.
Buffalo, NY 14224

First published in Great Britain in 2021 by
The Watts Publishing Group



**Credits**
Editor: Izzi Howell
Designer: Dan Prescott, Couper Street Type Co.

The publisher would like to thank the following for permission to reproduce their pictures:

Alamy: Goran Bogicevic 25t; Getty: serpeblu 5b, MR1805 7b, Daniel Eskridge 11b, mj0007 19t, Warpaintcobra 20; Martin Bustamente: 15c, 24; Shutterstock: Herschel Hoffmeyer cover, 4r, 5, 7t, 10, 15b, 16 and 17, Warpaint title page, 9, 12, 18, 23b, 26 and 27t, Catmando 4l, 11t, 13, 22 and 28, First Step Studio 6, Elenarts 8, Puwadol Jaturawutthichai 14, Daniel Eskridge 15t, dcwcreations and Martin Leber 19b, ODM 21, Andreas Wolochow 23t, Linda Bucklin 27b, John Wollwerth 29.

All design elements from Shutterstock.



Printed in the United States of America

CPSIA compliance information: Batch #CSGS26: For further information contact Gareth Stevens at 1-800-542-2595.



## PRONUNCIATION GUIDE

*Allosaurus* (AL-oh-saw-rus)
*Archaeopteryx* (ark-ee-OPT-er-ix)
*Argentinosaurus* (AR-gent-ee-no-SORE-us)
*Baryonyx* (bah-ree-ON-icks)
*Carcharodontosaurus* (car-CAR-oh-don-toe-sore-us)
*Carnotaurus* (car-no-TORE-us)
*Coelophysis* (seel-OH-fie-sis)
*Compsognathus* (comp-sog-NATH-us)
*Dakotaraptor* (dah-CO-ta-rap-tor)
*Deinonychus* (die-NON-i-kuss)
*Diplodocus* (DIP-low-DOCK-us)
*Giganotosaurus* (gig-an-OH-toe-SORE-us)
*Hesperornis* (hess-per-ORN-iss)
*Megaraptor* (MEG-ah-rap-tor)
*Microraptor* (MI-crow-rap-tor)
*Ornitholestes* (or-nith-oh-LES-teez)
*Shantungosaurus* (shan-TUN-go-SORE-us)
*Spinosaurus* (SPY-no-SORE-us)
*Stegosaurus* (STEG-oh-SORE-us)
*Tarbosaurus* (TAR-bow-SORE-us)
*Therizinosaurus* (THER-ee-zine-oh-SORE-us)
*Triceratops* (tri-SERRA-tops)
*Tyrannosaurus rex* (tie-RAN-oh-SORE-us recks)
*Velociraptor* (vel-OSS-ee-rap-tor)
*Yutyrannus huali* (you-ty-RAN-us HOO-ah-lee)

# CONTENTS

# MEET THE

DINOSAURS CAN BE SORTED INTO GROUPS THAT SHARE CERTAIN FEATURES. THEROPODS BELONG TO A CATEGORY OF DINOSAURS CALLED SAURISCHIANS, OR LIZARD-HIPPED DINOSAURS. THEROPODS WALKED ON TWO LEGS. NEARLY ALL OF THEM WERE KILLER CARNIVORES.

The first theropods evolved in the Late Triassic Period. They lived until the Late Cretaceous Period. Theropod fossils have been found on every continent except for Antarctica.

**LATE TRIASSIC DINOSAURS**

*Coelophysis*

**TRIASSIC PERIOD**
(252 to 201 million years ago)

**LATE JURASSIC DINOSAURS**

*Archaeopteryx*
*Allosaurus*
*Compsognathus*
*Ornitholestes*

**JURASSIC PERIOD**
(201 to 145 million years ago)

# THEROPODS

All dinosaurs, including theropods, were killed off in a mass extinction event 66 million years ago. Scientists believe that this event may have been triggered by a giant asteroid hitting Earth in the area known today as Mexico. The impact of the asteroid released huge amounts of dust and gas, which filled the atmosphere and changed the climate on Earth, making it too cold for dinosaurs to survive. However, other prehistoric species did survive, such as early mammals, fish, reptiles, and the descendants of theropods–birds (see pages 26–27).

**EARLY CRETACEOUS DINOSAURS**

*Yutyrannus huali*
*Baryonyx*
*Giganotosaurus*
*Microraptor*
*Deinonychus*

**LATE CRETACEOUS DINOSAURS**

*Tyrannosaurus rex*
*Spinosaurus*
*Velociraptor*
*Tarbosaurus*
*Therizinosaurus*
*Dakotaraptor*
*Carnotaurus*
*Megaraptor*
*Carcharodontosaurus*

**CRETACEOUS PERIOD**
(145 to 66 million years ago)

# SMALL AND LARGE

**THEROPODS CAME IN A RANGE OF SIZES. THE FIRST THEROPODS WERE SMALL, BUT OVER TIME, LARGER SPECIES EVOLVED AND BECAME HUGE, POWERFUL KILLERS.**

Early theropods, such as *Coelophysis* (see pages 12–13) were lightweight and agile. They had thin bodies and long, narrow heads. Their small bodies allowed them to run fast and chase down prey. As theropods became larger, they didn't lose their speed. Instead, they developed other features that helped them to move quickly, such as large, muscular legs (see pages 18–19).

Smaller theropods were often the prey of larger theropods.

It's hard to know which species of theropod was the largest. Only a few bones have been found from some species. Paleontologists (scientists who study fossils) can use these bones to estimate the size of the dinosaur, but it's not a guarantee, as individual dinosaurs were different sizes.

*Carcharodontosaurus* was one of the largest theropods. At 50 feet (15 m) long, it was almost the length of a bowling alley!

Later, bird-like theropods (see pages 26–27) evolved and became smaller again. This made them a better size for flight. Birds' small size could be one of the reasons that they survived the mass extinction event that killed the dinosaurs, as they didn't require as much food.

*Microraptor* was a small, bird-like theropod. It only measured around 2.5 feet (80 cm) long.

# SORTED:

## COMPSOGNATHUS

**QUICK FACTS**

**PERIOD:**
Late Jurassic

**LIVED IN:**
Europe

**LENGTH:**
2–3 feet (60–90 cm)

**WEIGHT:**
12 pounds (5.5 kg)

**THIS TINY DINOSAUR IS ONE OF THE SMALLEST KNOWN THEROPODS. IT WAS ONLY AROUND THE SIZE OF A CHICKEN. HOWEVER, IT WAS A FIERCE PREDATOR, AND SPEED AND AGILITY WERE ITS TOP WEAPONS.**

### AGILITY

*Compsognathus* used its long tail for balance as it swerved to chase prey. This agility gave it the winning edge during the hunt for equally nimble lizards and small mammals.

### SMALL BODY

*Compsognathus* weighed very little due to its small size and skinny body. It may have also had hollow bones like a bird. *Compsognathus*'s low weight helped it to run quickly when hunting prey and escaping predators. It may have been able to reach speeds of over 37 miles (60 km) per hour.

### DINOMIGHTY!

A fossil of an ancient lizard has been found inside the fossil of a *Compsognathus*, providing rare direct evidence of which species *Compsognathus* ate.

# SPINOSAURUS

**THIS MEGA DINOSAUR WAS PROBABLY THE LARGEST LAND CARNIVORE EVER, AS WELL AS THE LARGEST THEROPOD! ITS BODY WAS ADAPTED FOR HUNTING FISH AND OTHER WATER ANIMALS, BUT ITS HUGE SIZE WOULD HAVE ALSO ALLOWED IT TO OVERPOWER AND KILL OTHER LAND DINOSAURS.**

## QUICK FACTS

**PERIOD:**
Late Cretaceous

**LIVED IN:**
North Africa

**LENGTH:**
46–60 feet (14–18 m)

**WEIGHT:**
26,500–44,000 pounds (12,000–20,000 kg)

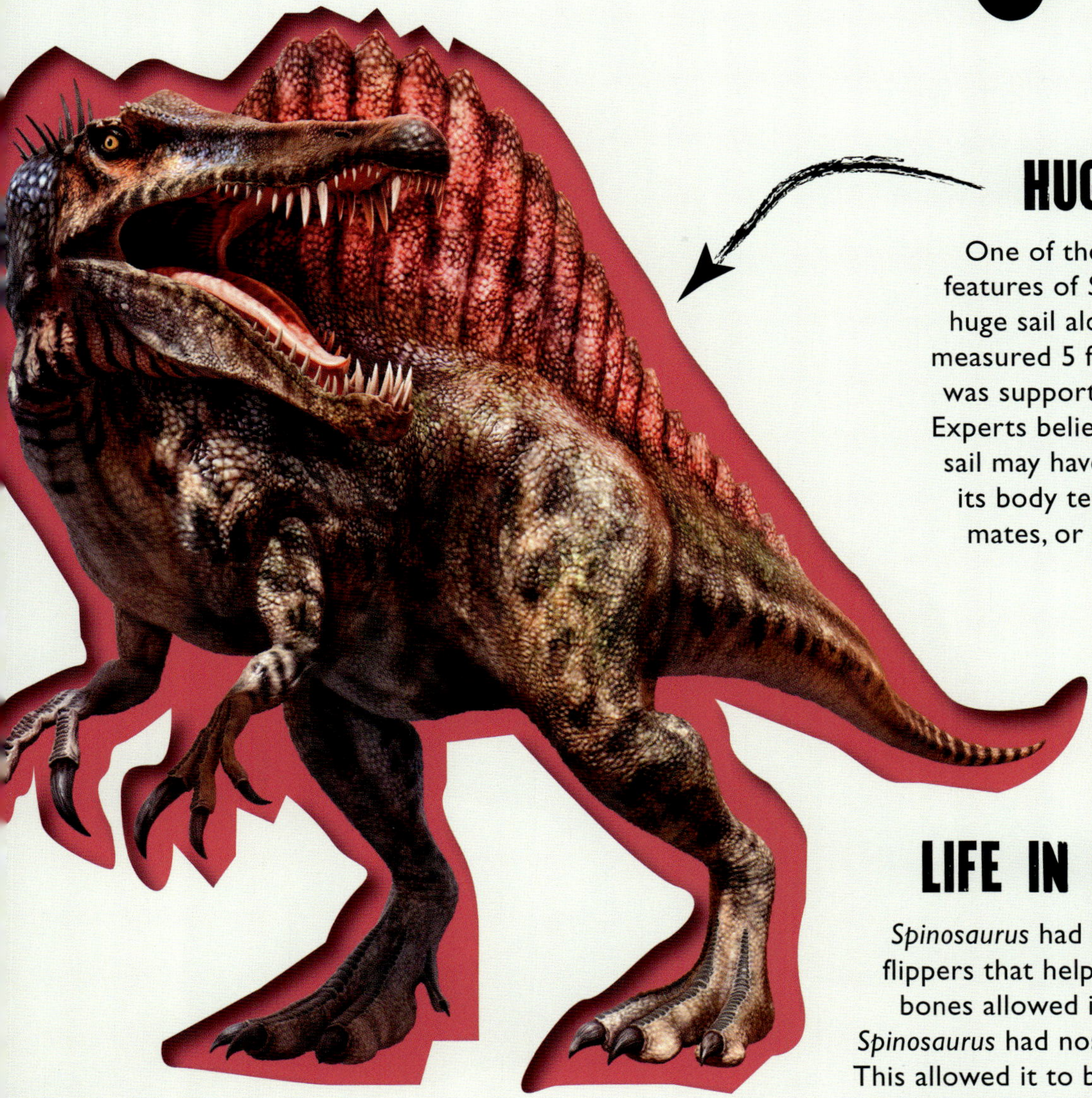

## HUGE SAIL

One of the most distinctive features of *Spinosaurus* was the huge sail along its back. Its sail measured 5 feet (1.5 m) long and was supported inside by bones. Experts believe that *Spinosaurus*'s sail may have helped to control its body temperature, attract mates, or scare its enemies.

## LIFE IN THE WATER

*Spinosaurus* had paddle-shaped feet like flippers that helped it to swim. Its dense bones allowed it to float in the water. *Spinosaurus* had nostrils halfway up its snout. This allowed it to breathe while the tip of its jaw was underwater. Inside its mouth were rake-like teeth that it used to trap fish.

# PREDATORS

**MOST THEROPODS WERE FEARSOME PREDATORS. THEY HUNTED AND ATE OTHER ANIMALS FOR FOOD.**

Prehistoric animals and plants were part of a food web, just as they are today. Some small theropods were in the middle of this web. They ate smaller animals, but were often the prey of larger dinosaurs. Other theropods, such as *Giganotosaurus*, were apex predators. These dinosaurs were so large and powerful that they faced almost no risk from any other animal.

*Giganotosaurus* may have hunted *Argentinosaurus*, one of the largest ever land animals. Both species lived during the Cretaceous Period, in the area that is today Argentina.

Most theropods ate a wide range of prey, including other dinosaurs, reptiles, amphibians, and insects. A few species of theropod were omnivores. They ate plants as well as meat. One group, the therizinosaurs, are believed to have mostly eaten plants.

*Therizinosaurus* had a beak for eating leaves. Its terrifying 3.3-foot- (1-m) long claws were used as protection from predators.

Many theropods hunted and killed their prey, but some, such as *Allosaurus*, were probably also scavengers. They ate animals that were already dead–killed by old age, illness, or an attack from another animal.

*Allosaurus* may have hunted in packs.

# SORTED:

## COELOPHYSIS

**THIS EARLY THEROPOD WAS SMALL IN SIZE, BUT A FEROCIOUS HUNTER. ITS AGILITY AND SPEED MADE IT AN EXCELLENT PREDATOR.**

### AGILITY

*Coelophysis* had a long, flexible neck that could form an S-shape or straighten out entirely. This helped it to grab small prey that often hid behind trees or rocks. Its long tail provided balance when twisting and turning to follow prey during a chase.

### QUICK FACTS

**PERIOD:**
Late Triassic

**LIVED IN:**
North America, southern Africa

**LENGTH:**
up to 10 feet (3 m)

**WEIGHT:**
40–50 pounds (18–23 kg)

## WEAPONS

*Coelophysis* had hundreds of sharp teeth in long jaws that could reach into holes and burrows to snatch prey. While its back legs gave it the speed to catch its prey, its smaller arms grasped and held its victim while *Coelophysis* attacked with its teeth and claws.

## DINOMIGHTY!

*Coelophysis* has traveled into space! In 1998, the skull of a *Coelophysis* was taken to the Mir space station on a space shuttle. Later, it was returned to Earth.

## PACK HUNTING

Over 1,000 *Coelophysis* skeletons were discovered together at a site in New Mexico. Some paleontologists believe that this is evidence that *Coelophysis* lived and hunted together in packs. They may have worked together to target and bring down larger prey.

## SPEED

Like most other theropods, *Coelophysis* had hollow bones. This reduced its overall weight so it could move faster without using too much energy. Its strong back legs, with powerful muscles, gave it a boost of speed to overtake slower prey.

# TEETH AND JAWS

**PALEONTOLOGISTS LOOK AT THE SHAPE OF A DINOSAUR'S TEETH TO IDENTIFY WHAT KIND OF DIET IT HAD. IT'S CLEAR FROM THE THEROPODS' STRONG JAWS FILLED WITH RAZOR-SHARP TEETH THAT THEY WERE VICIOUS CARNIVOROUS HUNTERS.**

Theropods' teeth never became blunt, as they regularly fell out and were replaced throughout their lives. They used their teeth to attack their prey and to cut meat from bones. However, they didn't use their teeth for chewing. Meat is very easy to digest, unlike plants, so theropods could swallow it whole. The meat was broken down and digested in their stomach and intestines.

This is the fossilized skull of a *Tyrannosaurus rex* (see pages 16–17), containing its jaw and many of its teeth.

Different theropod species had differently shaped teeth and jaws, depending on the type and size of prey that they ate.

*Velociraptor*–As it was quite a small dinosaur, speed was key to overpowering its prey of small mammals and reptiles. It had narrow jaws and very sharp teeth.

*Baryonyx*–This dinosaur hunted fish in wetlands and rivers. Its teeth were pointed so it could spear fish. Its high nostrils allowed it to breathe while its mouth was underwater.

Theropods attacked their prey using a method known as "puncture and pull." First, they sunk their sharp teeth into their prey. Then they closed their mouth and pulled their heads backwards to rip away meat.

This *Tarbosaurus*, a theropod similar to *Tyrannosaurus rex,* would have used the puncture and pull technique to take down a *Shantungosaurus*, a plant-eating dinosaur.

# SORTED:

## TYRANNOSAURUS REX

THIS MIGHTY THEROPOD LIVED UP TO ITS NAME, WHICH MEANS "KING OF THE TYRANT LIZARDS" IN GREEK AND LATIN. ITS TERRIFYING TEETH AND POWERFUL JAWS COULD EASILY SLICE THROUGH MEAT AND BITE THROUGH BONE.

### QUICK FACTS

**PERIOD:**
Late Cretaceous

**LIVED IN:**
North America

**LENGTH:**
up to 45 feet (14 m)

**WEIGHT:**
15,400 pounds (7,000

### DINOMIGHTY!

Pieces of bone have been found in fossilized *Tyrannosaurus rex* dung (coprolites), which reveals that it swallowed bone fragments as well as meat.

## TEETH

*Tyrannosaurus rex* had 60 serrated, cone-shaped teeth, which measured up to 7.8 inches (20 cm) long. They were stronger than the teeth of other theropods. *Tyrannosaurus rex* used its teeth to kill its prey and cut meat into smaller pieces.

## JAWS

The bite of a *Tyrannosaurus rex* is estimated to have been three times more powerful than a lion's! A bite this strong required strong jaw muscles. A *Tyrannosaurus rex skull* had extra space to fit in these muscles. Once it had bitten off a piece of meat, it swallowed it whole, eating up to 500 pounds (230 kg) of meat in one bite.

## PREY

*Tyrannosaurus rex* used its excellent sense of smell to find live prey to kill and eat. It also scavenged for dead animals. As well as smaller prey, *Tyrannosaurus rex* was able to overpower large herbivores, such as *Triceratops*. It attacked the neck of its prey first so that the prey would quickly lose blood and not be able to escape.

## ATTACKS

Paleontologists have identified marks on *Tyrannosaurus rex* bones as bite marks from other *Tyrannosaurus rexes*. This may have come from fights over food or territory, or *Tyrannosaurus rex* may have been a cannibal and eaten its own species.

# POWERFUL LIMBS

**THE LEGS, FEET, AND ARMS OF THEROPODS HELPED THEM TO REACH TOP SPEEDS AND HUNT DOWN THEIR PREY. THIS IS ONE REASON WHY THEY WERE SUCH FEROCIOUS HUNTERS.**

Theropods walked on their hind legs. Their legs were extremely muscular, which boosted their speed during chases. They used their large tails to help them balance as they swerved from side to side following their prey.

Based on the size of its leg bones and muscles in its tail, experts believe that *Carnotaurus* may have been one of the fastest theropods.

Theropods ran on their front three toes. We often see their distinctive footprints preserved in rock. They did have a fourth toe at the back or the side of each foot, but this didn't leave an impression in the ground as theropods didn't put their weight on it when running.

Dinosaur footprints, such as these three-toed theropod tracks, can give us information about dinosaur behavior. For example, we can use the distance between footprints to calculate the dinosaur's stride length and speed.

Although theropod arms appear small and useless, they actually had an important function–holding on to prey so it couldn't escape. Theropods had three or four fingers on each hand and sharp claws to tear through meat.

An *Allosaurus* claw

A *Megaraptor* claw

# SORTED:

## ALLOSAURUS

**THIS HUGE THEROPOD WAS FIRMLY AT THE TOP OF THE LATE JURASSIC FOOD CHAIN. EVEN LARGE SAUROPOD DINOSAURS WOULD HAVE BEEN NO MATCH FOR ITS SUPER SPEED, SHARP TEETH, AND GIANT CLAWS.**

### ARMS

*Allosaurus*'s tiny forearms were less than 35 percent of the length of its back legs. However, they were strong. *Allosaurus* clung on tight to its prey with its powerful arms and sharp, curved claws, making it very hard for its victims to escape.

### QUICK FACTS

**PERIOD:**
Late Jurassic

**LIVED IN:**
North America, North Africa, southern Europe

**LENGTH:**
40 feet (12 m)

**WEIGHT:**
3,000 pounds (1,400 kg)

### LEGS

*Allosaurus* had strong back legs and could run at up to 20 miles (33 km) per hour. It could outrun and prey on large, slow dinosaurs, such as young *Diplodocus* and *Stegosaurus*, as well as other smaller dinosaurs.

### FEET

Like all theropods, *Allosaurus* walked on two legs and ran on its toes. It had a very small fourth toe on the inside of each foot.

## HEAD

*Allosaurus* had a large head and dozens of sharp, serrated teeth. However, its bite wasn't particularly strong and was weaker than that of modern crocodiles and lions. Paleontologists believe that instead of biting its victims, *Allosaurus* may have used its head as an axe, slamming its teeth into its prey and tearing off chunks of meat.

▲ We can see from the skeleton of *Allosaurus* that its eyes were in the front of its head. This gave it better vision to work out distance and timing during an attack.

**DINOMIGHTY!**

Like most dinosaurs, *Allosaurus* had a relatively small brain compared to the size of its body. Its brain was around the size of a loaf of bread, making it about as smart as an ostrich!

# FEATHERED REPTILES

**THE FOSSILS OF SOME THEROPODS HAVE REVEALED THAT THEY HAD FEATHERS. THEROPODS ARE THE ONLY TYPE OF DINOSAUR THAT HAD TRUE FEATHERS.**

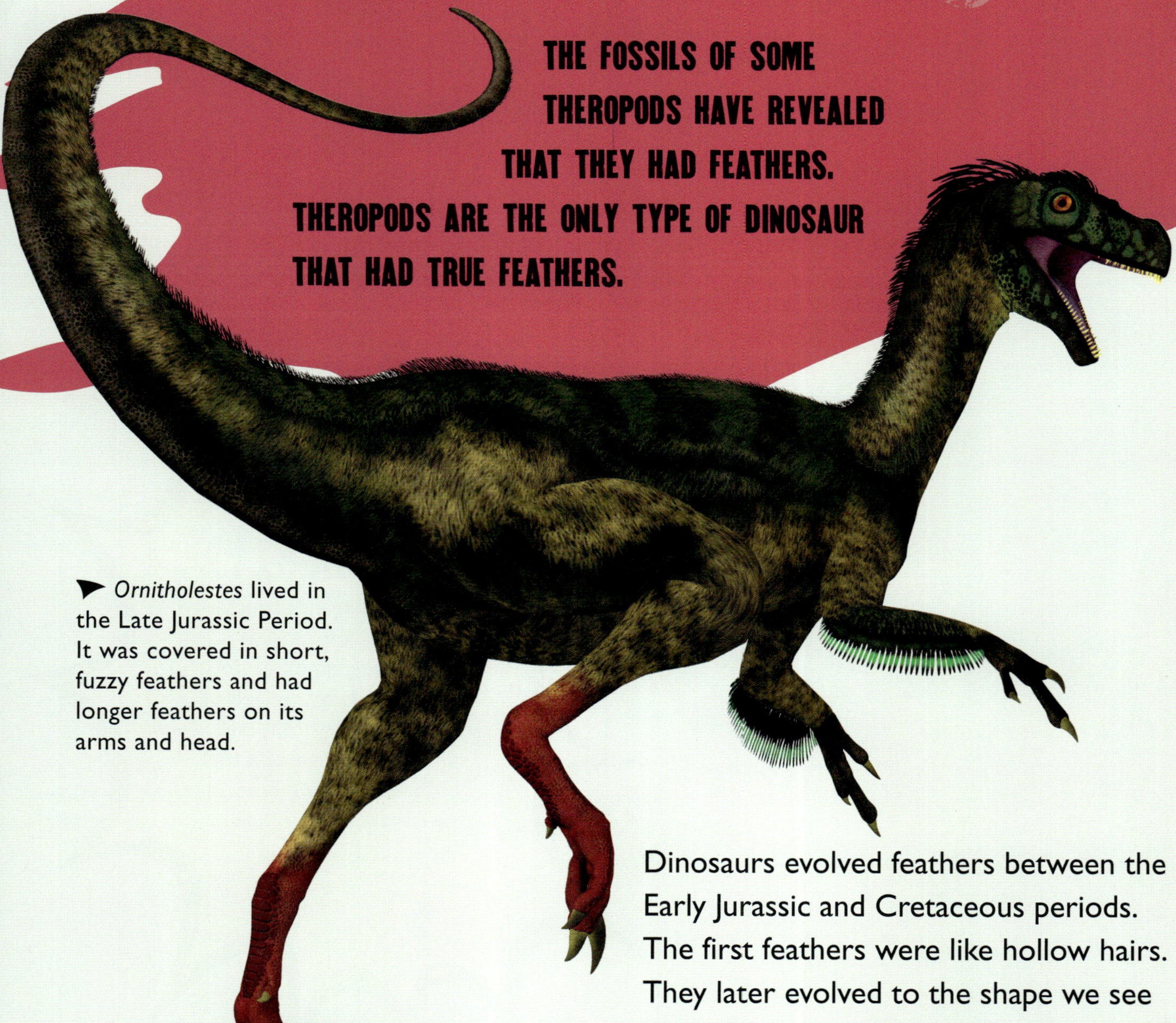

➤ *Ornitholestes* lived in the Late Jurassic Period. It was covered in short, fuzzy feathers and had longer feathers on its arms and head.

Dinosaurs evolved feathers between the Early Jurassic and Cretaceous periods. The first feathers were like hollow hairs. They later evolved to the shape we see today on modern birds, with tufts coming out of a long shaft in the center.

Feathers have allowed us to identify the colors of certain dinosaurs. This is because tiny pigment molecules are preserved in fossilized feathers. Scientists can extract these molecules to work out the color of the feather. They have found black, brown, gray, and reddish feathers.

A fossilized feather

Some dinosaurs had feathers on their tails and arms. These arm feathers were an early version of birds' feathered wings. Tail and arm feathers weren't used for flight at first. Instead, dinosaurs used these feathers to attract a mate, keep warm or cover and protect their young.

*Dakotaraptor* had large feathered wings. At 16 feet (5 m) long, it was too big to fly.

# SORTED:

## YUTYRANNUS HUALI

**THIS RELATIVE OF *TYRANNOSAURUS REX* (SEE PAGES 16–17) WAS THE LARGEST FEATHERED DINOSAUR AND THE LARGEST KNOWN FEATHERED ANIMAL EVER! *YUTYRANNUS HUALI* LIVED EARLIER THAN *TYRANNOSAURUS REX* AND MAY HAVE SHARED SOME SIMILAR FEATURES.**

### QUICK FACTS

**PERIOD:**
Early Cretaceous

**LIVED IN:**
China

**LENGTH:**
310 feet (9 m)

**WEIGHT:**
3,000 pounds (1,400 kg)

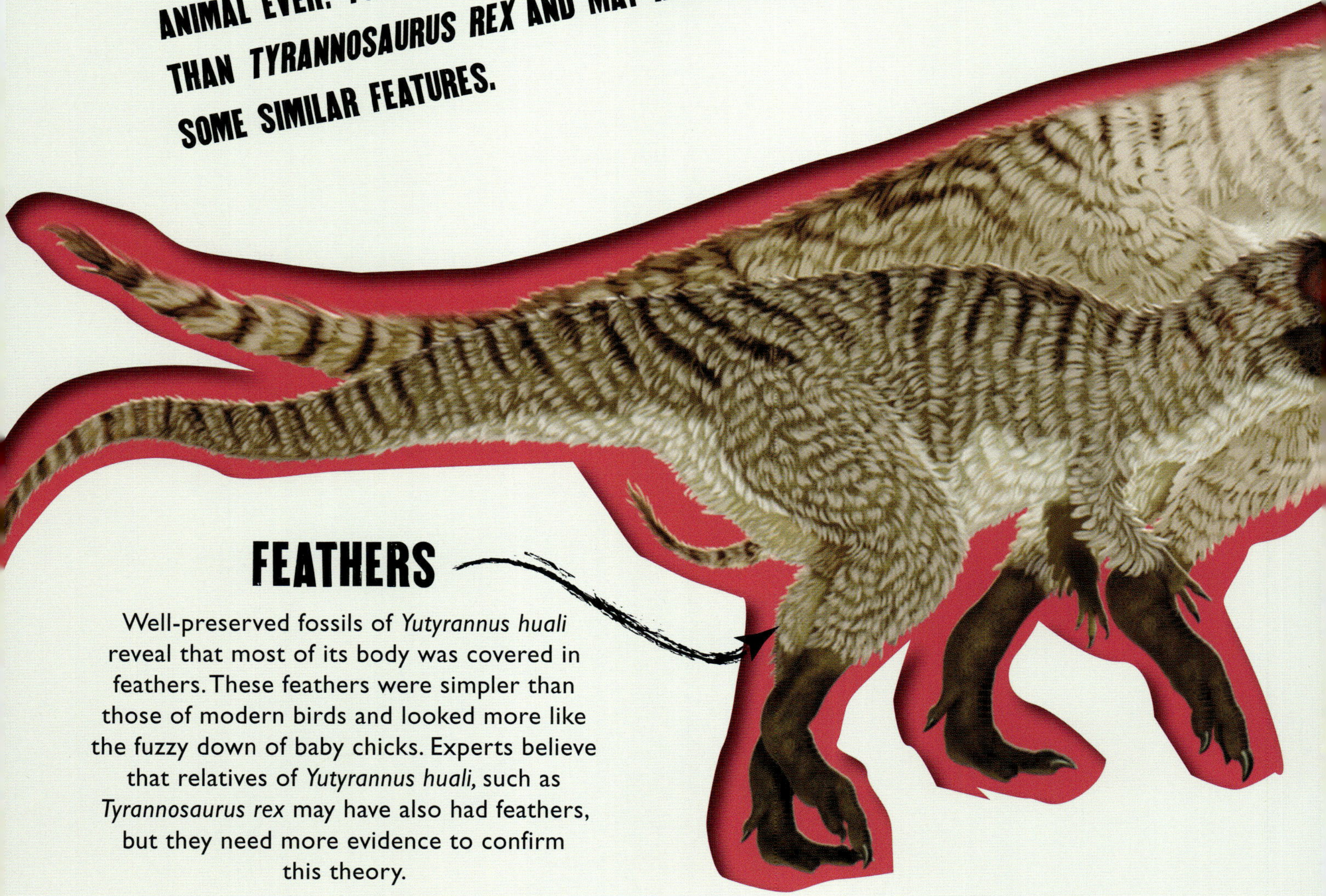

### FEATHERS

Well-preserved fossils of *Yutyrannus huali* reveal that most of its body was covered in feathers. These feathers were simpler than those of modern birds and looked more like the fuzzy down of baby chicks. Experts believe that relatives of *Yutyrannus huali,* such as *Tyrannosaurus rex* may have also had feathers, but they need more evidence to confirm this theory.

## FEATHER FUNCTION

*Yutyrannus huali* was too large to fly, so its feathers served another purpose. They probably helped it to stay warm in the cool climate of the Early Cretaceous Period. It could have also used its feathers to keep eggs warm in the nest, as camouflage, or to attract a mate.

This model of *Yutyrannus huali* is covered with replica feathers.

## FOSSILS

*Yutyrannus huali* was identified as a new species in 2012 when three nearly complete fossils were found in the same quarry in China. They date back approximately 125 million years. The fossils are from an adult, a smaller adult, and a young dinosaur. This group formation could be evidence that *Yutyrannus huali* hunted in packs.

## CREST

From the fossils of *Yutyrannus huali*, we can see that the adults had a crest on their nose. This was probably used for display and attracting a mate.

## DINOMIGHTY!

The name *Yutyrannus huali* comes from the Mandarin Chinese word "yu," which means feather, and *tyrannos*, meaning tyrant in Latin. "Hual" means beautiful in Mandarin Chinese, so its full name is "beautiful feathered tyrant."

# DINOSAUR TO BIRD

**IN THE JURASSIC PERIOD, SOME THEROPODS BEGAN TO EVOLVE AND DEVELOP BIRD-LIKE FEATURES AS WELL AS FEATHERS. THESE BIRD-LIKE DINOSAURS WERE THE EVOLUTIONARY LINK BETWEEN DINOSAURS AND BIRDS.**

▲ *Deinonychus* gripped and killed its prey with its large claws. It often killed other dinosaurs.

Bird-like dinosaurs still had some typical dinosaur characteristics, such as jaws filled with razor-sharp teeth. Modern birds don't have teeth; they have beaks instead. Bird-like dinosaurs also had long tails.

Bird-like dinosaurs also had features in common with birds, including long wings and feathers (see pages 24–25). However, not all dinosaurs with feathers were relatives of birds. Some bird-like dinosaurs could fly, but paleontologists aren't sure if they were strong fliers. They may have just glided from tree to tree.

*Microraptor* had feathers on its legs and wings, some of which measured up to 7.8 inches (20 cm)!

In the Cretaceous Period, the first true birds evolved. Unlike dinosaurs, they had a short tail and no, or much smaller, teeth. Eventually, they evolved to have beaks. These birds survived the extinction event that wiped out the dinosaurs and are the ancestors of the birds that are alive today.

*Hesperornis* was a Late Cretaceous seabird that lived on fish. It couldn't fly, but it could dive underwater to catch prey, just like a penguin.

# SORTED:

## ARCHAEOPTERYX

**THIS BIRD-LIKE DINOSAUR WAS PART OF AN EVOLUTIONARY STAGE BETWEEN DINOSAURS AND BIRDS. *ARCHAEOPTERYX* WAS AROUND THE SIZE OF A CROW, AND IT LOOKED A BIT LIKE ONE TOO, AS IT HAD BLACK FEATHERS.**

### QUICK FACTS

**PERIOD:**
Late Jurassic

**LIVED IN:**
Germany

**LENGTH:**
20 inches (50 cm)

**WEIGHT:**
2.2 pounds (1 kg)

### TEETH AND CLAWS

Like other theropods, *Archaeopteryx* had sharp, pointed teeth, which it used to eat small reptiles and insects. Its feet had large, spiky claws to catch and rip apart prey. Unlike modern birds, which can't move their claws individually, *Archaeopteryx* could move each toe separately.

### TAIL

Another feature that *Archaeopteryx* shared with theropods was its long, bony tail. This had rows of feathers on each side, with longer feathers at the tip.

## WINGS

*Archaeopteryx*'s wings were long enough for short flights, but the dinosaur's anatomy shows that it may not have been a strong flier. It couldn't raise its wings very high because of the way its shoulder joints worked. *Archaeopteryx* didn't have a large breastbone to produce the power needed to flap its wings and fly for longer periods.

The outline of the wings and tail feathers of *Archaeopteryx* can be seen in this fossil. We have learned a lot about *Archaeopteryx* from several extremely well-preserved fossils.

## DINOMIGHTY!

The first *Archaeopteryx* fossils were found just a few years after Charles Darwin published his theory of evolution by natural selection. These fossils were proof of Darwin's theory that living things changed gradually over time into new species, for example, certain dinosaurs evolved into birds.

## HABITAT

At the time that *Archaeopteryx* lived, its habitat in the area that is now Germany had many islands surrounded by shallow seas. *Archaeopteryx* may have been able to fly from island to island, looking for food or escaping predators. Or it may have only managed short flights, flying up into trees to rest at night or to chase flying insects to eat.

# GLOSSARY

**ADAPTED** – changed to suit a particular environment better

**AGILITY** – able to move quickly and easily

**APEX PREDATOR** – a predator at the top of the food chain, with no known predators

**ASTEROID** – a large space rock that orbits the sun

**CARNIVORE** – an animal that only eats meat

**CREST** – a growth of feathers, fur, or skin along the top of an animal's head

**DENSE** – containing lots of matter in a small space

**DOWN** – soft, fluffy feathers, such as those found on a young bird

**EVOLVE** – to change and develop gradually over time

**FOOD WEB** – the way in which living things are connected by relying on each other for food

**FOSSIL** – the shape of something that has been preserved in rock for a very long time

**HOLLOW** – empty on the inside

**MASS EXTINCTION** – a period in which many species of living things die and stop existing

**MATE** – a reproductive partner

**NIMBLE** – able to move quickly and with precision

**OMNIVORE** – an animal that eats both meat and plants

**PACK** – a group of animals that live and hunt together

**PALEONTOLOGIST** – someone who studies dinosaurs and prehistoric life

**PIGMENT** – a substance that gives something else a particular color

**SCAVENGER** – an animal that eats dead animals that it has not killed itself

**SERRATED** – with a row of sharp points

**SPECIES** – a group of living things that are closely related and share similar features

# FURTHER INFORMATION

## BOOKS

*T. Rex vs. Anklylosaurus: Prehistoric Showdown*
By Tom Jackson (Lerner Publications, 2026)

*Why? Dinosaurs*
By Stephanie Warren Drimmer (National Geographic Kids, 2025)

## DRAW YOUR OWN

Use the information in this book to design a new theropod species. Remember to include all the features of theropods. Then give your dinosaur a name.

## WEBSITES

*www.natgeokids.com/uk/discover/animals/prehistoric-animals/t-rex-facts*
Discover 10 terrifying facts about *Tyrannosaurus rex*.

*www.nhm.ac.uk/discover/why-are-birds-the-only-surviving-dinosaurs.html*
Find out more about how dinosaurs evolved into birds.

*www.nhm.ac.uk/discover/dino-directory.html*
Explore different species of theropod in the Dino Directory.

# INDEX